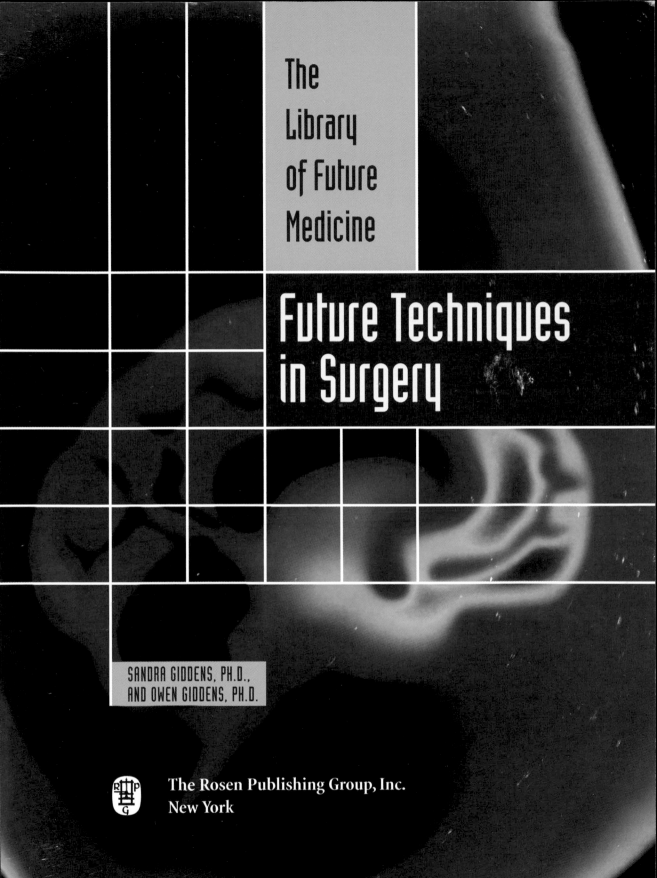

The Library of Future Medicine

Future Techniques in Surgery

SANDRA GIDDENS, PH.D.,
AND OWEN GIDDENS, PH.D.

The Rosen Publishing Group, Inc.
New York

Published in 2003 by The Rosen Publishing Group, Inc.
29 East 21st Street, New York, NY 10010

Copyright © 2003 by The Rosen Publishing Group, Inc.

First Edition

Library of Congress Cataloging-in-Publication Data

Giddens, Sandra.
Future techniques in surgery / Sandra and Owen Giddens.— 1st ed.
p. cm. — (The library of future medicine)
Summary: Reviews the evolution of medical surgery during two hundred years and predicts new procedures that may lead to greater safety and efficacy.
ISBN 0-8239-3667-8 (lib. bdg.)
1. Surgery—Juvenile literature. [1. Surgery. 2. Medicine.] I. Giddens, Owen. II. Title. III. Series.
RD31.4 .G53 2002
617—dc21

2001005598

Manufactured in the United States of America

Cover image: Surgeons perform angioplasty by inserting a catheter into a patient's groin.

Contents

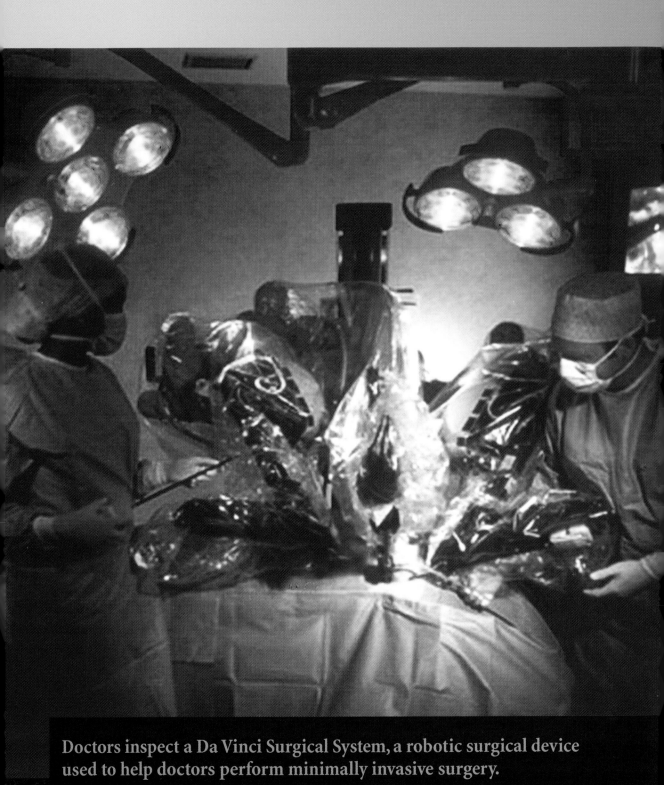

Doctors inspect a Da Vinci Surgical System, a robotic surgical device used to help doctors perform minimally invasive surgery.

Introduction

It was 1963. I was ten years old, and I was in the hospital. I had been probed, x-rayed, and tested to discover the cause of the pain that I was experiencing. On this day I had come to undergo exploratory surgery. I was wheeled into the operating room. There were adults all around me, gowned from head to foot. I thought, as I looked around me, that I had become a character in one of those scary science fiction television shows I had grown up watching. I was now the one being abducted by aliens.

The anesthetist put a mask over my face and had me breathe in deeply. He said to count backward from ten. I had not gotten too far in my counting when I became completely unconscious. When I woke up after the operation, I felt that someone had stuffed my mouth with cotton balls. My mouth was so very dry. I discovered when I looked down that I had a scar line about four inches in length on my

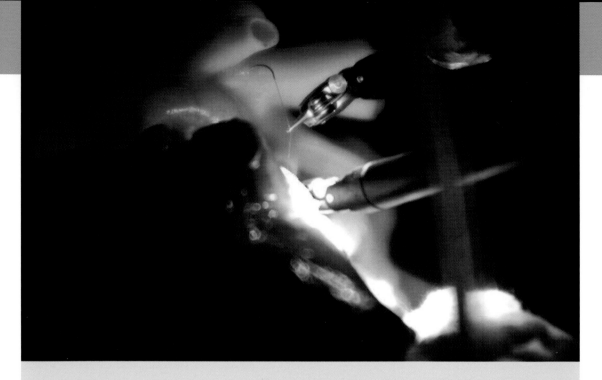

This robotic surgical device is operated by a doctor who sits at a separate control panel.

abdomen, and I was told that my appendix had been removed. It took a long time for the anesthetic to wear off. It took many days until I was finally released from the hospital and allowed to go home.

Now let's fast-forward to one day in the future. In the hospital of the future, I would lie down while a machine scans my body and determines the cause of my pain. I would be given a minimal amount of anesthetic or a pain blocker. A computerized robotic arm programmed by a surgeon would operate on me, and I would leave the clinic the very same day. I would look down and see only a microscopic trace of a scar. How far are we from this scenario? Not as far as you might think.

Surgery has evolved quickly in a very short time. It is difficult to imagine how much more advanced it will be in the future as each day brings new innovations in medicine. In order to understand the evolution of surgery, one must take a journey back in time to understand how we got to where we are today, and then zoom ahead into the future where one is limited only by his or her imagination.

Sandra Giddens

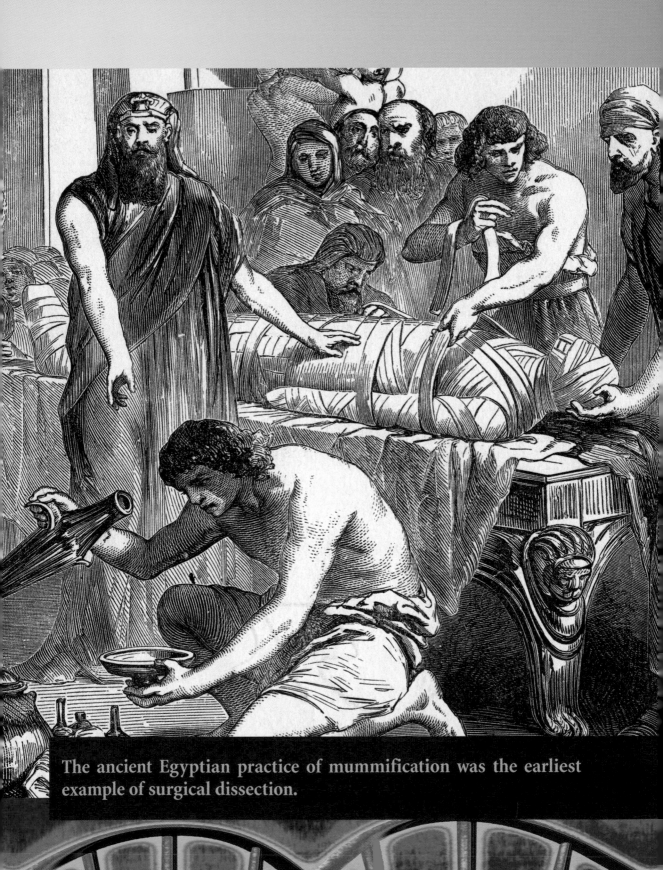

The ancient Egyptian practice of mummification was the earliest example of surgical dissection.

Surgery Past

Surgery has been with us throughout the ages. If we took a journey back to prehistoric times, we might enter a cave and watch the first operation on the brain. The caveman who was being operated on would not be under any anesthetic. In fact, the person would be alert and conscious. The person conducting the operation would make a hole in his patient's head with a stone ax or a rock knife. This procedure was called trephining, and we believe that it was used to help patients with headaches or to let out the evil spirits from the heads of people who were thought to be possessed. We know that trephining was done in the past because fossil hunters have discovered the preserved bones of Neanderthal cavemen from the Stone Age and some of these skulls had holes in them.

Approximately 4,500 years ago, the ancient Egyptians were preserving dead bodies, which we call mummies, with embalming fluids and potions. The process of mummification included the removal of the brain in pieces through the nose, as well as taking out the lungs, guts, and other inner organs through an incision in the side of the body. The body was then treated with salts, herbs, and special fluids. Many of the bodies were wrapped in cloth bandages, and many preserved mummies are seen in museums today. This certainly was the beginning of surgical dissection.

About 2,400 years ago, there lived a famous Greek physician by the name of Hippocrates. Hippocrates believed that nature healed all wounds and the physician was part of that

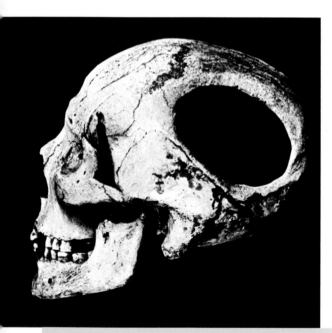

natural healing process. He felt that sometimes the doctor did not need to do anything and that the body would heal itself. The doctors and surgeons of that time were not consistent in their advice and treatments. They kept no medical records, and some of their methods were so dangerous

The hole in this Stone Age skull indicates that the person underwent trephining surgery.

that the cure was worse than the illness, so many patients died. Hippocrates devised a set of guidelines for doctors to use. These guidelines included talking to patients, examining and testing to identify the problem, and giving treatments sensibly. He felt that keeping records was a necessity.

In Roman times, about 2,100 years ago, the great physician Galen, who considered himself the successor of Hippocrates, treated gladiators and slaves who fought in the famous Colosseum. He believed that an understanding of anatomy was essential for a doctor. He was a master of dissection, most likely on animals as it was illegal to perform dissections on humans. He wrote many books about anatomy, and his influence lasted hundreds of years.

In Europe during the Dark Ages, from about AD 400 to AD 800, there was hunger, pestilence, and war. The Church of Rome was the only safe haven for the sick. The monks kept records, but they did not concern themselves with medical theories. The Dark Ages opened the door for false treatments involving charms and amulets. Medical learning and experimentation came to a halt. Saint Benedict, born in AD 480, was the exception. He encouraged monks in his monasteries to study medicine. He emphasized the study of Hippocrates and Galen. In these monasteries, medical education grew and flourished.

Around 1300, the Renaissance began in Europe, and there was a gradual revival of scientific learning. The study of anatomy was aided by the artist Leonardo da Vinci, who drew spectacular illustrations of bones, muscles, and other body parts with a degree of accuracy not seen before. The physician Andreas Vesalius published *On the Structure of the Human Body* in 1543. Vesalius performed his own dissections of animals and also human bodies. Human dissections were still frowned upon during the Renaissance, but Vesalius performed them anyway, and he corrected many of the errors and misconceptions of those earlier anatomists who could work only with animals. For example, it had been believed that men had one less rib than women because the Bible said that Eve had been created from one of Adam's ribs. Vesalius disproved that notion. The modern age of anatomy had begun.

In 1628, William Harvey, an English physician, wrote the book *On the Motion of the Heart and Blood*, and this revolutionized the medical thinking of the day. Harvey theorized that blood was pumped by the heart all through the body. Previously, many people believed that blood was produced in the liver and absorbed by the body. Now the circulation of the blood through the arteries and veins was understood.

CONTROLLING PAIN

Over the centuries, numerous techniques have been used to dull sensation for surgery. People in surgery were held down, knocked out, or given alcohol until they were very drunk. Bleeding patients into unconsciousness was another method that was tried. Before the middle of the nineteenth century, laudanum, a mixture of opium and alcohol, was the only agent regarded as of practical value in diminishing the pain of operations. Unfortunately, the large doses of alcohol could cause nausea, vomiting, and even death, and the opium was typically not powerful enough to completely dull the sensation of a sharp surgical tool entering the body. Many times the patient woke up during surgery and experienced excruciating pain. Charles Darwin wrote in his autobiography about surgical procedures he had witnessed:

> I also attended on two occasions the operating theater in the hospital at Edinburgh, and saw two very bad operations, one on a child, but I rushed away before they were completed. Nor did I attend again, for hardly any inducement would have been strong enough to make me do so; this being long before the blessed days of chloroform. The two cases fairly haunted me for many a long year.

A Boston physician who wrote about surgery before proper anesthetics were developed could only compare surgery to the Spanish Inquisition. He recalled, "Yells and screams, most horrible in my memory now, after an interval of so many years."

On October 16, 1846, William Morton, a Boston dentist, was the first to use ether to put a patient to sleep during an operation. Using a specially designed glass inhaler containing an ether-soaked sponge, Morton administered the anesthetic to Gilbert Abbott, a printer. John Collins Warren, one of the most widely recognized surgeons of that time, then removed a tumor from Abbott's neck. When Abbott awoke, he informed the audience that he had felt no pain. An item in the *People's Journal* of London reflected the excitement of this discovery:

> Oh, what delight for every feeling heart to find the new year ushered in with the announcement of this noble discovery of the power to still the sense of pain, and veil the eye and memory from all the horrors of an operation ... WE HAVE CONQUERED PAIN.

Local anesthesia was introduced in 1853, using morphine, followed by cocaine and novocaine. In 1885, Leonard

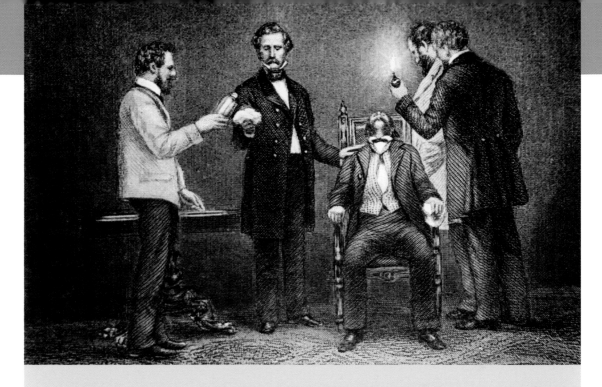

William Morton *(second from left)* demonstrates the use of ether to eliminate pain.

Corning, a surgeon from New York, experimented with spinal anesthesia, injecting a cocaine solution into the patient's spine.

There was, incredibly, a lot of resistance to efforts to eliminate the pain of surgery. Pain was often thought of in religious terms, as something that tested the righteous and punished the wicked. The Bible said that women should bring forth children in suffering. It wasn't until 1853, when Queen Victoria decided to give birth to her seventh child with the aid of chloroform, that the prejudice against painkillers died away.

CONTROLLING INFECTION

The prevailing view throughout most of history was that illness was spiritual in its origin. By the sixteenth century, scientists had some inkling that some diseases had causes external to the body. Although microscopes revealed the world of microorganisms in the seventeenth century, the link between germs and disease was not made. Chemist Louis Pasteur (1822–1895) finally made the link in the nineteenth century and used his skills with the microscope to identify germs. From his work with the microorganisms that cause fermentation in wine and beer, he hypothesized that disease arises from germs attacking the body, causing the decay of tissues. Many doctors refused to accept his theory at first. They found the notion of tiny organisms killing vastly larger ones to be absurd.

Joseph Lister (1827–1912), a professor of surgery at the Glasgow Royal Infirmary in Scotland, was deeply disturbed by the number of patients who died of infection after surgery. Even before the work of Pasteur, Lister had been convinced of the importance of cleanliness in the operating room. When he learned of Pasteur's research, Lister realized that the formation of pus was the result of bacteria, and he proceeded to develop antiseptic surgical methods. He treated instruments with carbolic acid, and he insisted that doctors and nurses wash their hands before surgery. The number of patients who died of infection dropped dramatically. Before the discovery of antiseptics, surgeons saw no need to wash their hands before operating on their patients, nor any need to sterilize surgical instruments or bandages.

In *Antiseptic Principle of the Practice of Surgery*, published in 1867, Lister wrote:

> I left behind me in Glasgow a boy, thirteen years of age, who between three and four weeks previously, met with a most severe injury to the left arm, which he got entangled in a machine at the fair ... Without the assistance of the antiseptic treatment, I should certainly have thought of nothing else but amputation at the shoulder-joint; but as the radial pulse could be felt and the fingers had sensation, I did not hesitate to save the limb.

Disease and simple infections killed many people before the discovery of antibiotics. In the nineteenth century, the average life expectancy was only about forty-seven years. This was because, though many people lived to ripe old ages, a great many children and young people died of infections and fevers. President Calvin Coolidge could do nothing for his sixteen-year-old son as the young man lay dying of septic poisoning from a simple blister on his toe. In 1928, Alexander

Fleming discovered that the mold he had grown could kill certain bacteria. He reported his findings in a medical journal, but this accidental discovery of penicillin was largely ignored.

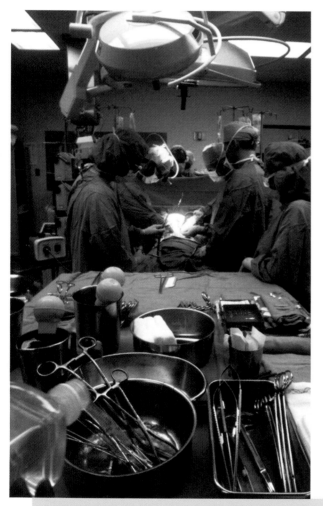

It wasn't until 1942, when a fire destroyed a nightclub in Boston in which hundreds of people were severely burned, that penicillin was rushed to the scene to treat the injured. The penicillin allowed doctors to perform skin grafts without contaminating the wounds with bacteria. Finally, in World War II, the government recruited more than twenty chemical companies to produce penicillin.

Antibiotics, however, remain one of the great medical problems of the

Today, the sterilization of surgical instruments is standard practice in operating rooms.

future. In the great game of evolution, microorganisms soon develop resistance to a particular drug. Today, there are many drug-resistant strains of diseases that just a few years ago we thought we had conquered. And the pace at which new antibiotics are developed has not been as rapid as hoped. New approaches may be required in the future.

DISCOVERIES OF THE PRESENT AGE

In 1879, William Macewan (1848–1924) ushered in the era of modern brain surgery. He operated to remove a blood clot from the brain of a patient. Surgeons were soon carrying out all kinds of brain operations. They had progressed a long way from those cavemen drilling holes in patients' heads!

As early as 800 BC, skin grafts were performed in India to conceal amputation of the nose. Amputations were done at that time as a punishment for adultery. In China, around AD 200, attempts were made to replace diseased organs with healthy organs, with little success. In the nineteenth century, organ and tissue transplants were performed on animals, but again most were unsuccessful. The first successful transplant of a human organ was the transplant of a kidney in 1954.

In 1895, the German physicist Wilhelm Roentgen announced the discovery of rays that could penetrate the soft

A technician demonstrates a device that maintains blood flow to a living kidney until it can be transplanted.

tissues of the human body and produce pictures of its internal structure on photographic film. He called these rays X rays. By the 1920s, X rays had become a regular part of medicine. In 1971, scientists combined X-ray images with a computer, taking hundreds of separate X-ray scans at slightly different angles to create a three-dimensional image of internal organs. This technique is called computerized axial tomography (CAT). A CAT scan lets your doctor see the size, shape, and position of structures that are deep inside your body, such as organs, tissues, or tumors. In 1984, magnetic resonance imaging (MRI) became available. This technique is especially useful in imaging the brain, spinal cord, the soft tissues of the body, as well as joints. MRI creates a strong magnetic field around you and then transmits radio waves to the area of your body to be pictured. The radio waves cause the hydrogen atoms in your tissues to resonate and emit their own radiation, which is detected and recorded by the MRI scanner. Because MRI scans exist as digital files in a computer, they can be manipulated to show a part of the body from different angles or even in three-dimensional form.

In the 1940s and 1950s, two rather important medical techniques had significant bearing on the development of cardiac surgery and on modern methods of treating disease. These were the use of hypothermia and the cardiac pacemaker.

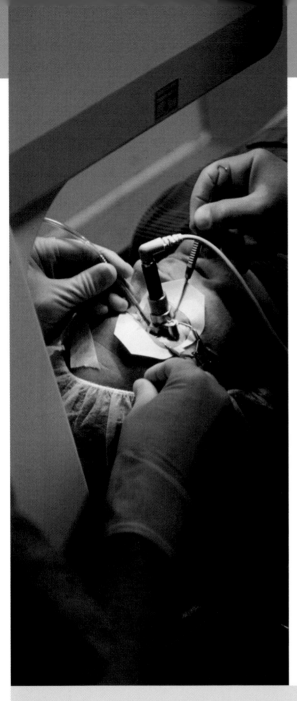

In 1941, the Canadian surgeon Wilfred Bigelow amputated a patient's frostbitten fingers. He complained to a superior that very little was known about frostbite. The senior surgeon suggested that Dr. Bigelow should make it his business to learn more. "For some reason that challenge hit home," Dr. Bigelow wrote. He developed an interest in hypothermia, the artificial reduction of the body's temperature to slow metabolic processes. The ability to slow the body's metabolism would prove essential for the development of open-heart surgery.

Doctors perform eye surgery. In earlier times, the manipulation of fine blood vessels in such organs was impossible.

In the 1970s, Dr. Svyatoslav Fyodorov of Russia was treating a boy whose broken eyeglasses had caused lacerations, or cuts, in the cornea of his eye. Following recovery, the boy's eyesight was less myopic than prior to his injury. This led Dr. Fyodorov to study the potential of refractive surgery, or surgery to alter the shape of the cornea and improve eyesight. In 1978, American ophthalmologists became interested in his findings. The laser has been used effectively since 1987 for this type of surgery. It is projected that in the early twenty-first century, millions of people in the United States will be treated with laser surgery to improve their vision.

The understanding of anatomy, antiseptics, anesthetics, antibiotics, X rays, and the function of the heart are just some of the advances that medicine has made over the past two centuries. We can now look at the techniques of present-day surgery and speculate on what we might see in the future.

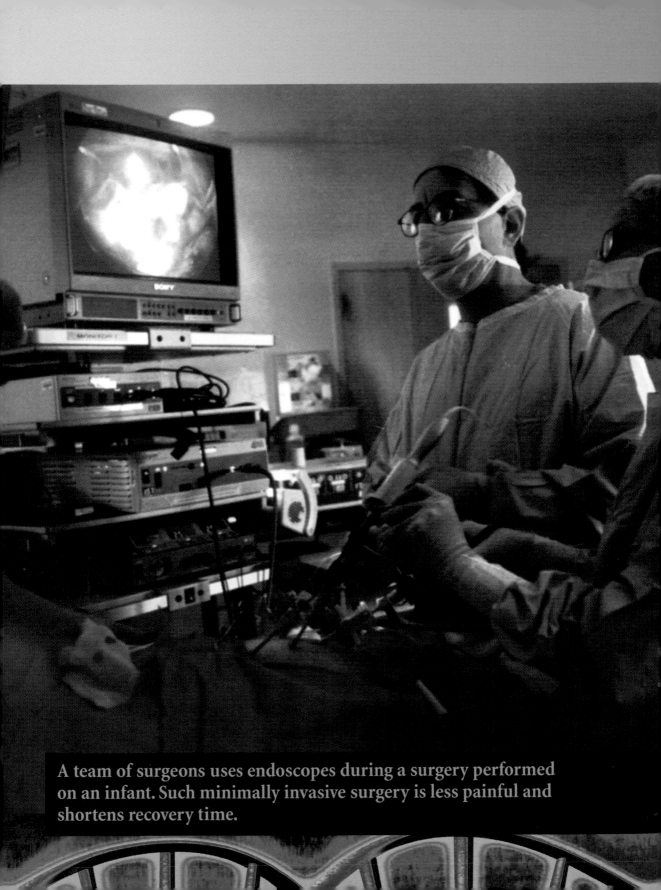

A team of surgeons uses endoscopes during a surgery performed on an infant. Such minimally invasive surgery is less painful and shortens recovery time.

2 ◇ Surgery Present

There has been amazing progress made in surgery in a great many areas. One of those areas is diagnostic accuracy. Surgeons today are guided by technology before operating on a patient. They have viewed the X rays. The ultrasounds, CAT scans, and MRI scans have already been interpreted, and the doctors can operate with full confidence that they know what and where the problem is.

Another area of improvement is the use of smaller surgical incisions. Smaller incisions produce less tissue trauma and reduce the risks to the patient dramatically. In minimally invasive surgery (MIS), the operation is performed with instruments and viewing equipment inserted into the body through small incisions created by the surgeon, in contrast to open surgery with large incisions. Endoscopic surgery uses small incisions and tiny instruments attached to fiberoptic viewing devices. The first practical endoscopic surgery was gallbladder removal. Operations that once required a long incision through the abdominal wall, a week's stay in the hospital, and six weeks recovery at home turned into outpatient procedures in which the patient was back to work in a couple of days. Today, in the United States, 600,000 gallbladder operations are performed annually, 95 percent of them endoscopically. Endoscopic surgery has even been used on fetuses in the womb to correct life-threatening birth defects before birth. These new techniques have reduced the risk of serious complications from brain surgery from almost 90 percent of patients in the 1940s to about 2 percent in the 1990s. Even the lighting in operating theaters has improved. With better lighting technology, the surgeon can look inside the patient with ease.

Better microscopes have improved medical diagnosis. Today, microscopes are a mainstay of pathology, the science of disease and abnormal health conditions. The ability to rapidly prepare and view sections of diseased tissue under high magnification assists the physician in determining the nature and extent of the medical problem. The electron microscope, first developed in the 1930s, can magnify objects up to one million times. Laser-scanning microscopes are giving doctors a glimpse into the physiology of living cells. Magnifying devices can now be worn directly by surgeons as they perform operations.

New tools to prevent or control bleeding have also been beneficial. The surgeon can stop bleeding reliably with the use of chemical clotting agents. By reducing bleeding, the surgeon has more time to work on the patient, so complex or critical procedures can be performed in a more orderly fashion, with less anxiety or room for error.

Surgical instruments have become much more sophisticated. For example, there are now electrically powered surgical instruments, as well as stapling instruments that can join

Ruben Quintero, the first doctor to perform surgery on a baby while it was still in its mother's womb, poses with some of the instruments he used during the operation.

blood vessels or other tissues in far less time than hand stitching. There are new advanced glues, surgical tapes, and even zippers that allow surgeons to close the patient without stitches.

There are, as well, many new surgical techniques. Cryogenic freezing of tissues allows surgeons to more precisely remove tissues and abnormal growths. Ultrasound, which uses very high frequency sound waves, can be used to break up kidney stones or scan the uterus of a pregnant woman. Medical lasers, which produce amplified monochromatic light waves in a very narrowly focused beam, have been used in eye surgery and have made it possible for individuals to experience freedom from total dependence on glasses and contact lenses. Laser vision correction is a general term that describes the use of the laser to improve vision by reshaping the contour of the cornea. A computer equipped with special software determines the exact pattern of laser pulses needed to improve vision.

Another exciting new area involves what are called intraoperative guidance systems. These systems can actually guide the surgeon as he or she operates. Specially adapted MRI devices allow the surgeon to see live images of what he or she is doing on a monitor during surgery. Three-dimensional images can be created using the data from the MRI scans and these images can be rotated to any position on a computer screen, or

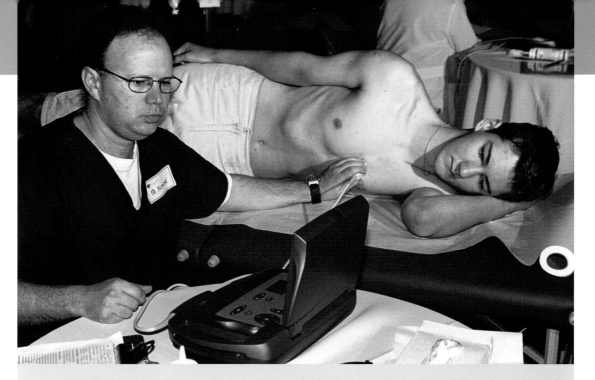

A cardiologist examines a patient's heart with a portable ultrasound machine.

layers of tissue can be digitally erased for a better view of underlying organs.

Surgery today routinely takes less time than in the past, and usually produces better results. Today we have new techniques to diagnose and repair parts of the circulatory system. We can monitor the heart's activity with electrocardiograms and ultrasound. We can implant pacemakers to adjust the heart's rhythm. We can start a stopped heart with defibrillators, and we can image the interior of blood vessels to look for blockages. We have an arsenal of drugs and surgical procedures to keep blood vessels clear or to create new routes for blood flow. Heart valves are being repaired and replaced, and

A county sheriff displays a portable defibrillator used to treat people who suffer heart attacks.

antihypertensive drugs are keeping blood pressure low to avoid straining the heart. We now have, or are close to having, artificial replacements for the heart.

CASE STUDIES

We will look at present-day surgery through the eyes of three doctors. Each has a unique historical perspective on their own specialty, and each makes an attempt to predict what the future holds in their area of medicine.

Dr. Martin Heller of Toronto, Canada, looks upon the future of medicine from the perspective of an orthopedic surgeon:

The training today to become an orthopedic surgeon consists of an undergraduate degree in the basic sciences, followed by medical school, residency, and four to six years of surgical training. Some doctors continue on with sub-specialty fellowships. For example, one surgeon may specialize in tumors of the spine alone.

I look at war, unfortunately, as advancing the treatment of trauma. There were so many amputations on the battlefield! Today, there are many advances that improve the treatment of fractures. A surgeon in the past would insert tons of screws and the limb would be stiff. Now we are minimally invasive and we let nature do as much of the healing as possible. In the past the patient would stay in the hospital for a longer period of time. Now many orthopedic cases are handled as same-day surgery.

I feel that there has to be an emphasis on teamwork in surgery nowadays. There has to be an accurate history taken of the patient, a proper physical examination, and an accurate diagnosis before surgery is to commence. The surgeon depends on experts in these fields to take good pictures and make accurate tests, and interpret the findings properly. In the prescreening process the patient may have the opportunity to meet the anesthetist and talk about any concerns he or she may have. In the operating room the nurses are very important. In some states there are physicians assistants present who are not doctors but are trained to help in surgery. After surgery, there is a recovery team to support the patient, and afterward, depending on the operation, the patient may go to a ward, go home, or receive additional support from social workers or physiotherapists. Surgery has to be well orchestrated. Everyone has to know his or her job in order for an operation to be successful.

The biggest improvement in surgery today is the use of minimally invasive techniques. For example, a knee ligament reconstruct is now same-day surgery, and immediately after discharge the patient is able to bear weight on his or her knee. The metal screws and pins used in surgery in the past have been replaced by bioabsorbable materials that will dissolve in the body. In shoulder surgery, technology is being developed to make smaller incisions. Therefore fewer muscles will be cut. With the advance of new technology, specialized training is essential for the surgeon.

Who knows, in the not-so-distant future we may be able to grow cells that can be injected into the body so that a new hip joint will grow!

Dr. Maurice Druck, a cardiologist from Toronto, Canada, says:

Before the 1940s we could not do heart surgery because the techniques weren't there. We did not have equipment for cooling the body, and we did not have a heart-lung bypass machine, therefore we could not stop the heart. The earliest heart surgery had to be closed heart surgery. The surgeon put his finger in the heart with a knife at the end of the finger to open the valve. The actual knife looked like a crochet hook. It was called a mitral knife. It is interesting to note that with closed heart surgery the mortality rate was less than 10 percent, which is low considering the lack of technology.

In the 1950s many men were dying from heart attacks, and there was little treatment for them. There were no high blood pressure pills and no cholesterol medicines. People were living badly, overeating and drinking excessively, and they had to be treated. Tissue cooling techniques and the bypass machine came into general use. In 1958, Dr. Mason Sones of the

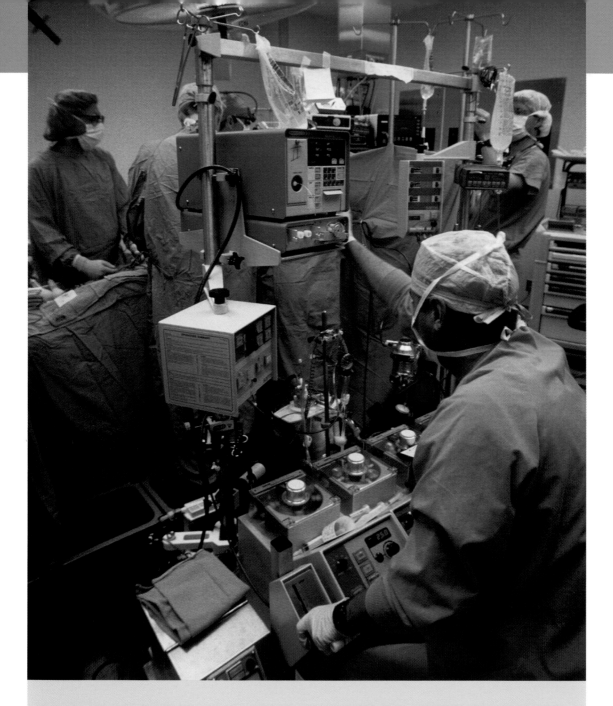

A doctor monitors a heart-lung machine, which pumps and oxygenates a patient's blood during a heart bypass operation.

Cleveland Clinic invented coronary angiography, which is a special X-ray procedure that takes pictures of the arteries. The radiologist watches a catheter, or tube, moving through the blood vessels on a special X-ray television screen. When the catheter reaches the site under investigation, X-ray dye is injected through the catheter. This clearly outlines the blood vessels and enables the radiologist to see any irregularities or blockages. Once the arteries can be seen, they can be repaired. The blocked arteries are bypassed to create new blood flow.

In 1964, the first bypass operation was performed. In this operation, a vein was taken from a leg and sutured to the damaged blood vessel above and below the blockage. The problem with these veins was that they did not last. They eventually formed blockages themselves, and therefore the medical field started to look for something else. In 1978, the internal mammary artery was being used for bypass surgery. Until the 1990s, only one mammary artery was being used and the rest of the bypass surgery utilized veins. Nowadays, it is possible to do bypass surgery using all arteries and as few veins as possible. The heart is stopped completely, and the heart and lung machine takes over for the whole body. The trend nowadays is not to stop the heart during surgery but to use a special machine called the octopus to keep the heart beating.

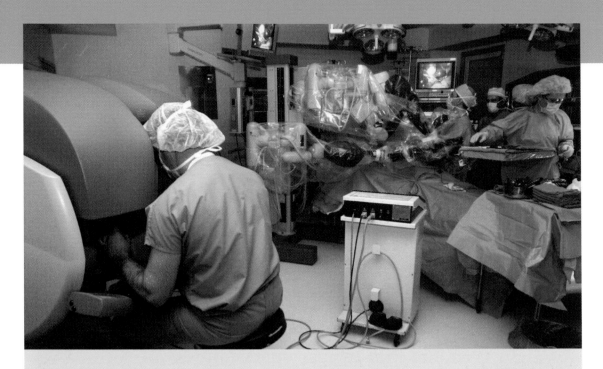

A surgeon manipulates the arms of a robotic device during a gallbladder operation from a control panel ten feet away.

There is now laparoscopic surgery. Laparoscopy is a method in which the inside of the patient can be visualized without making large incisions. Specially designed fiber-optic microscopes, measuring less than half an inch in diameter, are attached to high-resolution television cameras and inserted through very small incisions into the chest cavity. The advantage of laparoscopic surgery is that the chest of the patient does not have to be open and the patient can go home within forty-eight hours. There is a new procedure in which laparoscopic surgery is done by a robot guided by a surgeon standing in another room.

The exciting thing about all these new accomplishments in surgery is that when a new technique is accepted it is disseminated as soon as possible to surgeons all over the world. Today surgeons can also learn from live teleconferencing. In the 1980s, the average length of stay in the hospital for bypass surgery was eight days. By 2000, that was reduced to five to six days for uncomplicated cases and, with laparoscopy, to forty-eight hours. In the old days, the patient was in the ICU (intensive care unit) for two to three days, on a ventilator for twenty-four hours, and in recovery for five days. Nowadays the patient is in the recovery room for less than twenty-four hours, the breathing tube is pulled out immediately, and the patient is up and walking the next day.

New blood vessels that help oxygenate the heart in patients with obstructed arteries are now being grown in the lab. We now are doing transplants of entire body parts. In 1966, the first pancreas was successfully transplanted; in 1967, the first successful liver transplant; and 1981, the first successful heart-lung transplant. In 1982, Barney Clark received the first permanent artificial heart at the University of Utah. The heart functioned for 112 days. As of 2001, we now have a battery-operated artificial heart.

In performing heart valve surgery, the use of mechanical devices or animal tissue is not ideal. Using cells from the patient's own body and growing heart valves from compatible tissue is preferred. The survival rate for this kind of surgery nowadays is more than 75 percent. Unfortunately, we have more patients requiring heart transplants than available hearts. Right now we have the mechanical heart, but truly the way to go is to grow heart muscles. If we are able to grow new heart muscle, then there will be no need for heart transplants. Another thing that has reduced the need for heart surgery is the fact that there are good heart medications on the market. Heart disease continues to be a high-profile disease, therefore money for research continues to be made available.

There is, of course, an ethical question that one needs to ask. If a person is a heavy drinker and smoker and will not change his or her lifestyle after heart surgery, should that person be

This self-contained mechanical heart was implanted into a patient in July 2001. The patient lived for four months with the artificial heart, but then died of an unrelated illness.

placed ahead of someone who has not caused his or her own health risks? A related question that needs to be asked in the future is what happens if surgery becomes so routine that people have little incentive to change their lifestyles. Will they continue in their bad habits because there is a quick fix?

Dr. Stephen Miller, a dermatologist from San Antonio, Texas, says:

> If you go back hundreds of years into the past, surgeons were not necessarily medical doctors but dentists and even butchers. Techniques today are more efficient, and surgeons are better trained. There is now a strict certification system for surgeons, and credentials are checked carefully.
>
> A great explosion of technology and knowledge has been seen in the last twenty-five years. Endoscopic surgery is employed in all fields and just recently was used in heart bypass surgery. Within the past decade, endoscopes have been developed that are much smaller and have more working channels for the passage of surgical instruments. Instead of opening the whole abdomen, a cut an inch long is made and diseased tissue is removed. The advantages of endoscopic surgery include less disturbance of tissues, less chance of infection, and a faster

recovery period. A person could have his or her gall-bladder surgery on Friday and be back to work on Tuesday. In the past, a patient could be disabled anywhere from two to six weeks or more for gallbladder surgery. With endoscopic surgery, there is a smaller scar. By performing less-intrusive surgery, the risk of complications, like a hernia, can be reduced.

Surgery has also advanced because of better diagnostic tools. X-ray machines are more sophisticated. Ultrasound, the most used diagnostic tool, sends out and records sound vibrations to create an image. Ultrasound is so safe that it is used with pregnant women. Blood tests have become more exact. CAT scans, MRI, and endoscopy are all tools that assist the doctor to make the best diagnosis for the patient. One famous neurologist with forty years of experience, when he first saw the CAT scan, said, "No one will know how to do a proper neurological exam within ten years because of the CAT scan." We have even developed further with the MRI.

Some of the procedures that I do are chemical peels, CO_2 resurfacing, laser surgery, skin cancer surgery, and skin grafts. Laser surgery is a cosmetic cutting tool. It creates in most cases a bloodless

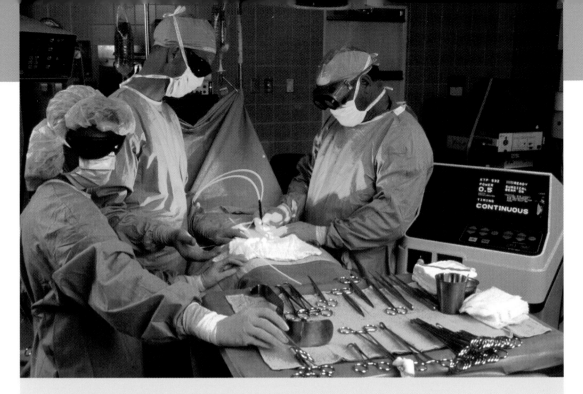

A team of surgeons perform laser surgery on a patient.

field to work on. The CO_2 laser is used for eyelid surgery. It reduces the recovery time and reduces the bleeding. There is less infection and consequently a faster healing time. I use the laser to remove skin pigmentation like birthmarks, sun damage, and tattoos. Lasers can also be used to permanently remove hair.

I see more and more neurosurgery advances. For example, the gamma knife is a precise cutting tool that uses gamma rays. It can be directed at tumors that we were not able to operate on in the past. The gamma knife was developed in 1968 by

This patient is about to undergo surgery by the gamma knife, which uses a beam of radiation to destroy diseased tissue.

Swedish professors Lars Leksell and Borge Larsson. It can be used to treat facial pain, benign and malignant brain tumors, and other brain disorders. What makes the gamma knife unique is that it successfully treats these conditions without incisions. It uses a concentrated dose of radiation from a pellet of cobalt-60. A total of 201 beams of radiation intersect to form a powerful ray focused on the target area of abnormal tissue. The gamma knife is so precise that it damages and destroys the unhealthy tissue while sparing the normal, healthy tissue.

In the future, the gamma knife will be adapted for use in most areas of the body. I also see more refined endoscopic surgery in the future. The benefits of less-invasive surgery are enormous. Transplant surgery continues to advance. More and more organs are being transplanted successfully. The antirejection drugs are better nowadays and these drugs will continue to improve in the future. Microsurgery has made huge advances. The reattachment of limbs has now become a reality. Nerves are invisible to the naked eye. With the development of surgical microscopes, these nerves are now visible.

I believe that the cost of surgery in the future may go down. It is very expensive to keep people in the hospital, and as surgery advances, patients may find more and more procedures performed on an outpatient basis, or hospital stays may be no longer than overnight. At this time technology is expensive, but in the future the cost may decrease.

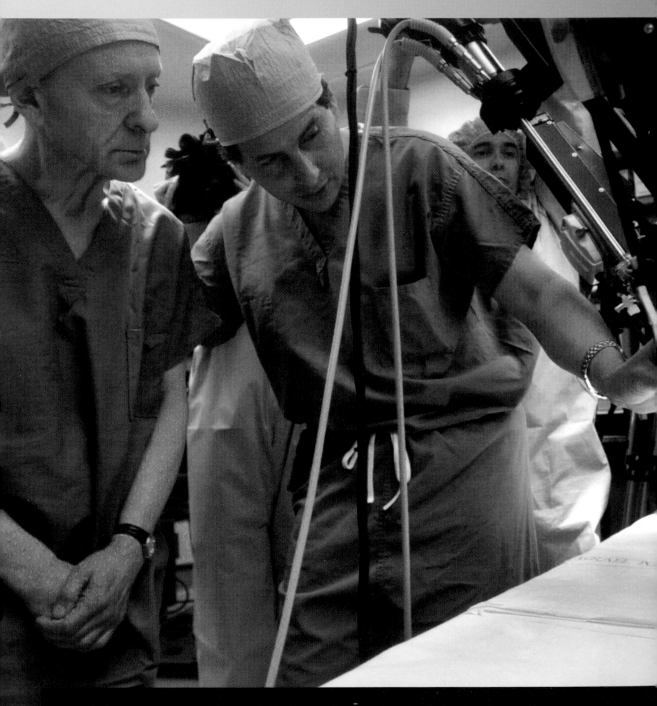

A doctor explains to his patient the robotic surgical device he will use in a coronary bypass operation to treat the patient's heart condition.

# 3 The Future of Surgery

The future of surgery is really difficult to predict, but there are new advances almost every day now in medical technology. We seem to have an insatiable desire to make things work better. There are some specific fields that are beginning to develop very rapidly. Robotics is one of those fields.

ROBOTICS

Today medical robots operated by computers are capable of amazing feats. These medical robots are busy in the laboratory and the operating room. In the operating room, a robot clasps a curved needle while another robot pulls the sides of a small coronary artery apart to get it ready for a graft. Together these robots make a dozen precise and delicate stitches in the heart before them. A third robot holds a camera steady next to the heart. The surgeon can watch the operation on a full-color television monitor in another room and give the robots instructions. These robots act as the surgeon's hands and eyes. Unlike the surgeon's hands, the robotic arms can grasp an eighteen-inch probe without causing even a slight tremor. Each robotic arm can adjust its own degree of movement to a millionth of an inch. The robotic camera can magnify the stitches by a power of sixteen.

In New Jersey, the Hackensack University Medical Center has been using a computer motion robot system known as AESOP. Recently, a surgeon there was busy operating on a patient. The surgeon made three incisions three millimeters long, small enough for Band-Aids to cover. He used a microphone and started talking to the robotic system. A fiber-optic camera smaller than a pencil was threaded into the patient's abdomen by a robot arm. "AESOP move left," the surgeon ordered. The robot chirped in response. "AESOP, stop," the surgeon called out after the robot had found the location to be repaired. "AESOP, get me some coffee," the surgeon said, then turned to the spectators and said, "That was a joke." The surgeon completed the surgery successfully with the aid of his robotic assistant.

Each surgeon cleared to use the AESOP system makes voice recordings. These recordings are used to make a voice card that is inserted into the robot so that AESOP can recognize commands. There is always a manual backup system if anything goes wrong. Robotic techniques can improve existing clinical procedures as well as provide innovative new approaches to current clinical problems. Robots are expected to make surgery safer and cheaper, and recovery much faster.

VIRTUAL-REALITY MEDICINE

A woman in a remote part of Minnesota suffers a severe wound in a hunting accident, but unfortunately a snowstorm prevents her from being transported to the closest surgeon. A doctor in a local clinic places the injured woman in a computerized mobile surgical unit. The unit's computers transmit her image to a surgeon in a St. Paul hospital. The surgeon dons a virtual-reality helmet that transmits to the surgeon scans of the patient made by the mobile surgical unit. Assisted by the doctor at the local clinic, the surgeon in St. Paul uses her hands to guide robotic instruments in the mobile surgical unit to operate on the wounded woman and save her life. This scene is not going to be imaginary for very much longer. Virtual-reality surgery, a vision out of science fiction, is just around the medical corner.

Virtual reality is already in use in diagnosing disease, in training medical staff, and in the operating room as well. Military surgeons are using virtual reality by simulating the repair of gunshot wounds to the legs and arms of virtual

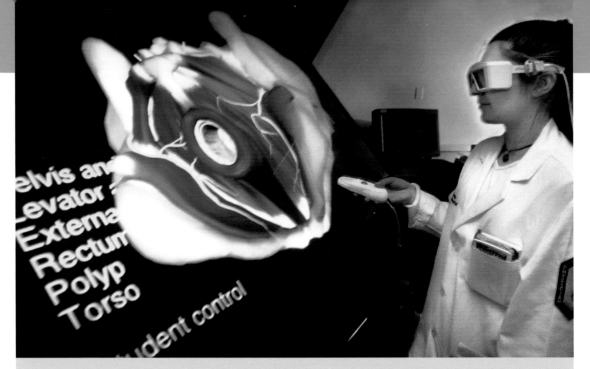

A surgical resident navigates through a 3-D projection of the human pelvis. Researchers are developing technology that will allow doctors to practice surgery on virtual organs before they begin operating on real ones.

patients. There is a virtual-reality training simulator for minimally invasive surgery. Surgeons and students can try different techniques and look at parts of the human body from perspectives that would be impossible during surgery. Virtual-reality technology will allow surgeons to rehearse operations before making a single cut, just as airplane pilots train on flight simulators, and medical students will be able to tour a 3-D version of the human body. Increased minia- turization of computers will allow tiny, sighted computers to be placed inside the body, where they will freely move about, diagnosing and repairing. As an indication of what the future may bring, on August 2, 2001, the *Toronto Star* filed this report:

> A pill-sized camera that is swallowed and snaps pictures as it travels through the digestive system won approval from U.S. regulators yesterday for helping doctors spot problems in the small intestine ... The camera can take pictures of the small intestine, a six-meter-long section that had been a "blind-spot" to current diagnostic tools. Patients swallow the camera, which looks like a pill capsule. It travels through the stomach and small and large intestines before being excreted from the body. On its way through, the device shines a light, takes two pictures per second, and transmits them by radio waves to a recorder worn on a patient's belt. Doctors transfer the digital images to a computer. They can view the images as still shots or run them together quickly like a video. The new camera should complement but not replace endoscopes, X rays, or other traditional diagnostic tools.

Surgeons have also expanded their operating teams to include radiologists, electronic engineers, bioengineers, computer engineers, computer programmers, and technicians. The techniques being developed today for the future are often referred to as "Nintendo medicine" because of their high-tech aspects. Open-body surgery will soon look as old-fashioned as sitting in a barber's chair to have a tooth pulled without anesthesia, a common practice a hundred years ago, does today.

STEM CELLS

There is a lot of excitement about President George W. Bush's statement in 2001 that there will be limited funding for stem cell research in hopes of finding cures for several major diseases. Bob Casper, head of reproductive sciences at Mount Sinai Hospital of Toronto, stated, "This really is tremendous. It really does have the potential to cure diseases that are currently incurable." What makes stem cells special is that they haven't yet formed into specific human cells, but are believed to be capable of "learning" how to become certain cells. Stem cells obtained from embryos, once isolated and cultured, can develop into any of the body's 220 tissue types. Researchers hope to repair or replace cells damaged by diseases or disabilities such as heart disease, Parkinson's disease, diabetes, Alzheimer's, and spinal cord injuries.

"If you are going to try to regenerate a liver for somebody, you may have to find a match among an embryonic stem-cell line," said Dr. Casper, but if doctors were able to harvest a person's own stem cells to grow replacement parts, there would be no concerns that a transplant would be rejected. Transplants of healthy heart muscle cells could provide new hope for patients with chronic heart disease whose hearts can no longer pump adequately. The hope is to develop heart muscle cells from human stem cells and transplant them into the failing heart muscle in order to augment the function of the heart. Preliminary work in mice and other animals has demonstrated that healthy heart muscle cells transplanted into the heart successfully repopulate the heart tissue and work together with the host cells. These experiments on animals show that this type of transplantation is feasible.

With donor organs so scarce, the next century will see new approaches. Scientists may be able to implant living replacement organs grown from single cells. In the future, with more sophisticated computers, doctors will be able to combine MRI, CAT, and other medical imaging devices to create a virtual you. There may be a time in the future when patients visiting their doctors will have their complete DNA profile on file, showing what diseases they may be susceptible to and what risks they may pass on to their children. In the future, there may be harvest banks for cloned body parts and stem cells.

The twenty-first century is an exciting century to live in. We are on the brink of discovering the causes of many diseases. One day soon we may be able to enter a clinic, be diagnosed through scanners, be operated on by robots, and walk out of the clinic on the same day.

Glossary

anatomy The physical structure of the human body; the science of the shape and structure of organs.

anesthesia The state of unconsciousness and loss of sensation usually brought about by drugs to eliminate the pain of surgery.

anesthetist A medical doctor who specializes in keeping the patient unconscious and free of pain during surgery.

angiography Examination of the blood vessels using X rays following the injection of a radioactive substance.

antihypertensive A substance that reduces or controls high blood pressure.

artery A blood vessel that carries blood away from the heart.

bioengineer Genetic engineer; a person who applies engineering principles to the fields of medicine and biology.

circulatory Relating to the circulatory system—the system consisting of the heart, blood vessels, and blood.

cornea   Outer layer of the pupil of the eye.

coronary   Of or relating to the heart.

cryogenic   Of or relating to low temperatures.

CAT scan   An image produced by a CAT scanner; a special radiographic technique that uses a computer to assimilate multiple X-ray images into two-dimensional cross-sectional images.

defibrillator   An electrical device that restores normal heartbeat by applying a brief electric shock.

electrocardiogram   A graphic record of the cardiac cycle.

endoscope   A long, thin metal rod with a fiber-optic camera at the tip.

ether   A volatile, flammable liquid with a sweet, pungent smell formerly used as an anesthetic.

fermentation   The conversion of sugar into alcohol by yeast.

graft   Living tissue, such as fat, skin, or bone, that is moved from one part of the body to another.

hypothermia   Abnormally low body temperature.

laceration   A jagged wound or cut.

laser   A tool that emits an intense, focused beam of light that can burn through flesh with more precision than a cut made with a scalpel.

liposuction   The surgical removal of fat deposits. It is one of the most popular cosmetic procedures performed in the United States.

microsurgery   Surgery on minute body structures or cells performed with the aid of a microscope and other specialized instruments.

monochromatic   Having only one color.

MRI Magnetic resonance imaging. MRI produces scans of body tissues by measuring the magnetic orientation of their atoms.

ophthalmologist A physician specializing in the treatment of the eye.

organism An individual form of life, such as a plant or animal.

orthopedic The branch of medicine that deals with the prevention or correction of injuries to the skeletal system and the muscles, joints, and ligaments.

outpatient surgery Surgery that permits the patient to return home the same day; also known as same-day surgery.

pathology The scientific study of the nature of disease and its manifestations.

physiology The study of the functions of living organisms and their biological systems.

probe An exploratory device designed to obtain information from a remote or unknown region.

refractive The turning or bending of a wave, such as a light or sound wave.

Renaissance The period of the rebirth of scientific learning and artistic creativity in fourteenth-century Europe.

robot A mechanical device that is capable of performing a variety of complex human tasks.

simulator A device that simulates, or imitates, actual or operational conditions.

stem cells Cells that have the ability to transform themselves into more specialized cells.

surgeon   A physician specializing in surgery.

surgery   A surgical operation or procedure, especially one involving the removal or replacement of a diseased organ or tissue.

transplant   To transfer tissue or an organ from one body to another.

trephining   The process of operating by using a trephine, a surgical instrument having circular, sawlike edges, used to cut out disks of bones, usually from the skull.

vein   A blood vessel that carries blood back to the heart.

virtual reality   A computer simulation of a real or imaginary system that enables a user to interact with that system.

X ray   A type of invisible ray that has great penetrating power. This means it can pass through soft body tissues such as muscles and intestines.

For More Information

ORGANIZATIONS

American Academy of Orthopaedic Surgeons
317 Massachusetts Avenue NE, Suite 100
Washington, DC 20002
(202) 546-4430
e-mail: DC@aaos.org
Web site: http://www.aaos.org

The American Association for Thoracic Surgery
Thirteen Elm Street
Manchester, MA 01944
(978) 526-8330
e-mail: aats@prri.com
Web site: http://www.aats.org

The American Board of Surgery
1617 John F. Kennedy Boulevard, Suite 860
Philadelphia, PA 19103
(215) 568-4000
Web site: http://www.absurgery.org

The American College of Surgeons
633 N. Saint Clair Street
Chicago, IL 60611-3211
(312) 202-5000
e-mail: postmaster@facs.org
Web site: http://www.facs.org

The American Society for Aesthetic Plastic Surgery
ASAPS Communications Office
36 West 44th Street, Suite 630
New York, NY 10036
(212) 921-0500
e-mail: media@surgery.org
Web site: http://www.surgery.org

American Society of Anesthesiologists (ASA)
520 North Northwest Highway
Park Ridge, IL 60068-2573
(847) 825-5586
Web site: http://www.asahq.org

WEB SITES

Due to the changing nature of Internet links, the Rosen Publishing Group, Inc., has developed an online list of Web sites related to the subject of this book. This site is updated regularly. Please use this link to access the list:

http://www.rosenlinks.com/lfm/futs/

For Further Reading

Guenst, Gary. *Surgery: What to Ask the Surgeon and More*. Skippack, PA: WCG Publishing, 1998.

Loftus, Jean M. *The Smart Woman's Guide to Plastic Surgery*. Chicago: Contemporary Books, 2000.

Parker, Steve. *Brain Surgery for Beginners and Other Major Operations for Minors*. Brookfield, CT: The Millbrook Press, 1993.

Rutkow, Ira M. *American Surgery: An Illustrated History*. Philadelphia: Lippincott-Williams & Wilkins, 1998.

Stutz, David R., and Bernard Feder. *The Savvy Patient: How to Be an Active Participant in Your Medical Care*. Yonkers, NY: Consumers Union, 1990.

Youngson, Robert M. *Surgery Book*. New York: St. Martin's Press, 1997.

Bibliography

Breuer, Hans, and B. J. Smit. *Proton Therapy & Radiosurgery*. New York: Springer-Verlag, 1999.

Ganz, Jeremy C. *Gamma Knife Surgery*. New York: Springer-Verlag, 1997.

Grace, P. A. *Surgery at a Glance*. Malden, MA: Blackwell, 1998.

Greulich, K. O. *Micromanipulation by Light in Biology & Medicine: Laser Microbeam and Optical Tweezers*. Boston: Birkhauser, 1999.

Lampert, Richard, ed. *Minimal Access Cardiothoracic Surgery*. Philadelphia: W. B. Saunders, 1999.

Rutkow, Ira M. *Surgery: An Illustrated History*. St. Louis, MO: Mosbey-Year Book, Inc., 1993.

Schein, Ed M., and L. Wise. *Crucial Controversies in Surgery*. Farmington, CT: Karger, 1997.

Index

Credits

ABOUT THE AUTHORS

Sandra Giddens has her doctorate in education. Presently she is a special education consultant for the Toronto district school board. Owen Giddens holds a doctorate in psychology. He is the director of Rehabilitation Counseling Services in Toronto.

PHOTO CREDITS

DESIGN AND LAYOUT

Evelyn Horovicz